APOLOGETIC

Apologetic

by Carla Funk

TURNSTONE PRESS

Turnstone Press
Artspace Building
206-100 Arthur Street
Winnipeg, MB
R3B 1H3 Canada
www.TurnstonePress.com

Turnstone Press gratefully acknowledges the assistance of the Canada Council for the
Arts, the Manitoba Arts Council, the Government of Canada through the Canada
Book Fund, and the Province of Manitoba through the Book Publishing Tax Credit
and the Book Publisher Marketing Assistance Program.

Cover design: Jamis Paulson
Interior design: Sharon Caseburg
Printed and bound in Canada by Friesens for Turnstone Press.

Epigraph on page ix is from "The Law That Marries All Things" by Wendell Berry.
© 1998 by Wendell Berry from The Selected Poems of Wendell Berry. Reprinted by
permission of Counterpoint.

Library and Archives Canada Cataloguing in Publication

Funk, Carla, 1974-
    Apologetic / Carla Funk.

Poems.
ISBN 978-0-88801-371-2

    I. Title.

PS8561.U8877A76 2010   C811'.54   C2010-901419-7

Mixed Sources
Cert no. SW-COC-001271
© 1996 FSC
FSC

Contents

I want to say a thing important and alive / 3

I.

II.

III.

~

Whatever is singing
is found, awaiting the return
of whatever is lost.

—Wendell Berry,
"The Law that Marries all Things"

Apologetic

I WANT TO SAY A THING IMPORTANT AND ALIVE

I want to pin the blueprint of a star behind the eye.
I want to bolt the worship of a stone within the brain,
screw the sea's long fermata to ventricle and valve.

A field of brome at twilight,
clearing crossed by deer, creek on hush,
abandoned orchard apple trees gone wild—
I want to push them all inside the blood.

Killdeer's call, wind's black howl,
that crush of moon-dragged waves on sand—
I want to lock them all inside the lung,
leave them kindling to speech,
honey in the carcass of a beast.

Words, like breath in winter,
manifest and vanish.
The body, too, a mist
that settles in the grass,
then fades. How quickly it lies down
beside the greenness of water,
how soon its shadow falls
under the anvil of the sun.

Though the world goes up in fire,
out of the skull of the village fool
dream-bleached and soaked in light,
burst all those common morphos,
blue wings flying up
through temporary darkness,
planet-tilt, interstellar hum,
back to the furnace and the cloud.

I.

SONGS OF THE HUMPBACK WHALE

Snowdrift night of childhood.
I lay on my bed listening to a square of black vinyl
torn from a nature magazine and on the hi-fi turning:
Songs of the Humpback Whale.

When I closed my eyes, the singing was
a girl in a well, a watery
photograph of sadness.

Floating south and blue, I descended
to the diver's hydrophone,
sinking in a pacific sea.

Then I was one of a million krill
swimming toward that song:

brine of leviathan's helixed keening,
variations on a local theme.

I rode that cavern echo, melodic
lows and highs breaching: *home, home.*

To everything a season,
to every season an end.
Inside, a singing comes.

Postlude, spat back to northern latitude,
I surfaced in a still dark world.
Trees bathed white. Snow hush.

From my broken sheet of ice,
I picked up the tune,
pitched my note to the hemisphere
and hummed along, singularly glowing.

In Fall

The children drag their feet
towards a life of clocks
and questions—
the day in fog,
pumpkin fields
on fire. Memory
scatters your path
with leaves
and broken twigs.

How many calendars ago
did your own mother
kneel before you
to button up your new coat,
bought two sizes too big
with room to grow?

Then her hands
were skilled and quick
as they folded down your collar,
brushed toast crumbs
from your cheek.

When she bowed
to lace your sneakers,
you saw the silver in her hair,
the beginning
of that other season,
one whose dusk
the body can't refuse—

black flowers on a drying vine,
burning oak, cricket song—
the old smoke waltz of autumn.

Early Autumn Cricket Song

Chaff-blown fields stubble up, horses in, haying done.
Miniature saws and hammers tear down the budding sun.

Reverb in the thistledown. A guild of scraping wings.
Tin itch and file. A pocket fiddle's resined strings.

Sings to instinct, to the rutted road, to the green sea.
Tinkers with the chafing breeze, drill-bit to the fir tree—

go dark, go dark. To rootwater, sap-sting, lulling pitch
and mossy branch. Quiet to quiet, stitch on stitch.

Let the drowsy bees bramble. Let the starling flocks fly
buckshot in the blue. Let the seedpods rattle and die.

Thrums on a fawn petal, a gilt-edged stalk. Chisels dust
from a lily's gold throat. The country of moth and rust

goes leaf-ash to the cloud. Unhinges from a dry blade
creaking, creaking. Then lays a red bent nail in the shade.

LITTLE ELEGY FOR AUGUST

When you left, I stood all morning
at the window, traced the rain,
waited for your whirr and flutter to return,
like the hummingbird to our plastic feeder
dripping sugar water, replica
of nectar in winter, which is what
happiness these days seems,
a thin syrup that anoints the tongue
with pleasure, then leaves,
like you, small and weathered
ghost of the potato patch and rosebush,
floating there in your gumboots
and your worn-out flowered dress.

Fox and Geese

At recess in the school field,
we tramped our circle in the snow
and boot-stamped spokes
to mark a wheel for our game
of fox and geese.

Always, the predator a boy
and we girls the prey.
We flew in shrieks and huddled
in the safety of the hub,
our no-kill zone.

The fox stalked stragglers first,
picked off the weak and slow,
ones fooled by easy plays
and those caught up in chatter.
Then moved in for the real hunt.

I wanted to be the girl
left running on the snowy track
while my captured sisters looked on
from their wintry cage, helpless.
I wanted to be the hold-out,

last one fending off the fox,
refusing nature. Be that girl who feels
his hands, his breath at my back,
but from the circle, breaks
for the cold, open field.

Evening Song

October falls away in shoddy patchwork,
gold scrap, sky a broken
arpeggio of wind-pitched starlings.

The complicated heads of deer raise
question marks in fog. Neighbourhood dogs
turn and turn, then stretch out in the sun's oily rags.

In the middle of the city, a lake opens its oval mirror
to trees—maple, oak, birch—all their flaming leaves
leaving flames to lick the water's fuel.

Against the coming starkness of bone, frost,
steel and stone, we back in, we cave up.
Early darkness shocks our bodies into faith.

Smoke rises from our shuttered house tonight
and you drop the needle on another dusty vinyl.
Scrape of leaves blowing down the road.

Intro to the first strains: two shaky violins
reaching to unhook high notes
from a bent and rusted wire.

COME WINTER

In this island city, snow comes
like an unexpected guest, the kind
you only hear from in holiday cards
and phone calls from the north, but now
out of nowhere, here he is on your front step
with a bottle of Chardonnay in one hand,
and a fruitcake in the other:
you don't know whether to open the door
or draw the curtains and hide.

Outside, the moon's a blur,
as if every star in the cosmos
has come loose from its moorings,
galaxies shaken out and falling.
Night gives up its darkness
to a pale blue glow. You sleep
in a world masqueraded by light.

Morning, you look out your window
and realize this is no dream.
Across the road, a snowman stares
back at you with one stone eye
and pebbles pressed into a half-smile.
With thin stick arms outstretched,
he could be a messenger sent
from some mysterious republic
to welcome you into this
monochrome land.

Down your front walk, you shovel
a way out, a way back to the familiar,
the greener world of rain and wind
and flying cherry blossoms.
In his own yard, your next-door neighbour
clears a path. Beneath his heavy coat and scarf,
and that toque pulled down to warm his ears,
he could be anyone—stranger, imposter,
undercover alien, like this world
you find yourself alive in,
this white planet, this winter city.
Hello, you call across the new quiet. Hello.

FUMBLING TOWARDS THE STAR

Beneath the backdoor exit's glowing red,
my father stood in stiff blue jeans, chewing
at a hangnail. Front row, my mother aimed
her broken camera.

      I was almost ten.
I wanted to be an angel. Instead,
I wore the plush head of a Christmas cow
with two holes cut for eyes so I could see
across the drafty church's stage to where
the swaddled Christ-child lay, that rubber doll
redeemed from someone's toy box and cleaned up
like everyone inside the sanctuary.

Shepherds came forth from the janitor's closet.
Down the centre aisle, wise men marched
in satin capes and paper crowns, fumbling
towards the tinfoil star nailed above our heads.
They brought what gifts they could: a velvet pouch
of something they called myrrh, a jewelry box
inlaid with gold, the cut-glass bottle of
an old perfume. The holy couple held
their pose, and stared into the manger straw.

From the balcony, a squad of angels
rallied down in bleached-out bed sheets,
handing out lit candles to everyone they passed,
including my father. He held the flame away
as if it were a trick, a stick of dynamite,
and he, a fool left hanging on in darkness
like me, onstage and waiting for my cue,
for everything to change.

I was almost ten.
I wanted to wear a silver halo,
a white robe. I wanted to stand inside
the glow and sing O Holy Night, to strike
another match in the weary, faithful crowd.
I wanted to sing my mother a new dress,
a new life, to bring my father to
the empty seat beside her, front row
where she waited.
                    The piano shimmered out
its starry notes, and angel voices hummed
their peace to every man. On hands and knees,
with all the other beasts, I crawled into the light.

Northern Crèche

Not to say their journey wasn't hard
but had that star floated over the Nechako
or settled at the peak of Sinkut Mountain,
how far would they have ridden out that weather—

sleet, black ice, a chill that splinters wind-lock
in the lung. Never mind their ocean crossing
leading up, shipwreck gales at the hull,
putting in at some bleak bay and hoofing it

by packhorse through canyon, past what-would-be
Hope, avalanche slide threat, the Fraser's flashing rapids,
through Spuzzum, Cache Creek, Cariboo country.
Mirage of frozen lakes, blizzard whiteout

blindness. Eyelids crusted shut, beards gone stiff
with frost, they'd wonder at the dream back home,
sun-fire over hills, the give of sand,
not this, not ponies frothing slump and weave

across nowhere Interior terrain.
That lit icon hacksawing darkness pitches
them to a leeside clearing in the spruce.
Into the aurora's ionic greening,

the star bleeds out heat, a hard shine making
plain a path broken in the wilderness.
These wise men bend to tracks cut fresh in snow:
claw and hoof hammered in the skiff

and chaining north, higher still. The fool's way
is an endless circle in the desert,
but here, under the warp of a polar sky,
the wandering toward eternity

is a trek through a wake of bent branches,
forward, ever towards, following
animals risen from forest thickets
as they shake off their winter sleep and go.

Winter Fire

As our bones grow old inside us
and our names in each other's mouths

go dim, we walk the frozen river
again to a windless clearing.

Here, we kneel and scrape back snow
to find bare ground, a place to build

a winter fire. With fuel gathered
from sheltered undergrowth, we ready

a tinder nest to take the spark
from our struck match. We bend, breathe

on an embering so faint, light
seems impossible. Beneath the ice

these blackest months, fish steel themselves
inside the drifting. They quiet

their blood, slow-hearted in the dark
waters we tread upon, enduring

a current washing and washing
silt out to sea. A cloud of incense,

our breath and smoke mingling, floats up
above this path cut through coldness,

above our heads. More than we can
fathom, this, this small fire burning.

Driving Past the Juvey

Ice and snow have slowed the cars to rush hour crawl
along the road that passes by the juvey.
Drivers can't help but look to where that building
jars the landscape, can't help but crane to see
the sealed windows and bolted gates.

Today, a white drift covers the basketball court.
Behind wire and chain-link, boys in grey sweatsuits
pelt each other with snowballs.
One takes a run and skids across the yard
as if it's any yard. Another's on his knees
scraping up what snow's blown in
through fence-hole and steel mesh.

Everything's disturbed. The sky
descends like ash of dying stars, filaments
of shadows turned against themselves.
Inside the pure and momentary light,
we drive towards houses strung with bulbs,
toward the flicker of trees, fire and glass.
Before it falls again to settle on the earth,
the clear and broken music shaken from our bones
ascends through dust, water, gold.

LATE WINTER

The new roof on the chicken coop.
Stacked firewood inside the shed.
A deep-freeze flush with meat and bread,
last summer's garden haul.

List all the things you're thankful for,
my mother says, and then the rest
won't seem unbearable.

The sheep that gave its fleece
to wool the winter quilt.
Northern lights that rush
the night in oils and gems.

Whoever takes the time
to count their blessings
takes away the hours
of discontent.

A single housefly crawls along the sill.
Outside the window, snowflakes
feather down the dark.

On the kitchen table,
a seed catalogue lies open
and circled in ink:
Millennium Asparagus,
Crimson Cherry Rhubarb,
and the Siberian Tomato,
prized for its sweet and early fruit.

THAW

First day of sunshine in a week and the world,
unlocked, begins again. Along the eaves,
icicles ignite, refract you in miniature,
standing like a miracle, blue against
whiteness. Snow tightroped on power lines
yields to the thaw, plummets to the road
limp-winged. A soundless falling from highwires,
then a cush of feathers disappearing,
vanishing in the fashion of a trick—
here, now gone with the weather's shift in tone.
The season of impossibility renders
a brilliance on things. Lets up enough
to drip light through you. The cold cracks
open a narrow door, and you, bent low, walk through.

WALKING UP GOVERNMENT STREET

On the other side of the tea shop window,
a woman lifts a clay cup to her lips,
steam wreathing her face.

Outside, cherry blossoms
blow in pink tornados at my feet,
swirl the curbs and stick
petals on a wet, black dog
leashed to a trashcan.

A yellow bicycle with a basket
and a polished silver bell
leans against a wooden bench.

Today I want to be the kind of person
who rides a yellow bicycle
with a basket full of bok choy
and fragrant pears. I want
to pedal across the blue bridge, ringing
my polished silver bell at strangers.
I want to annoy people
with my happiness.

Here, on a street floating with spring,
even store windows papered with old news
and the man sleeping below a stone lion
by the Chinatown gate—even they seem hopeful
in this wind of falling flowers.

Over the city, all the clouds of unknowing
let go the sky, surrender to this season's sugared rush.
Time scatters its petals on the street,
over the heads of strangers,
into the open hand of a girl who stands
with her mother under a polka-dot umbrella,
waiting for the light to change.

Spring Fling at the Holy Cross

They drag each other out to dance
beneath a spinning disco ball—

girls who've shunned their knee-length kilts
for strapless gowns and taffeta,

boys who've traded ties and slacks
for untucked shirts and baggy pants.

They sway and sweat inside a crush
of awkward limbs and cheap perfume

as is the lowly body's rite,
passage through a cruel season

strung with paper flowers, foil stars,
crepe streamers and balloon bouquets.

They are in the darkness shining.
Light varies blue and violet

on their faces, prisms their skin
with the mirror's fractured dazzle.

Above their heads, Christ hangs sad-eyed,
sorry as the boy who hunkers

in the bleachers for the evening's
few slow songs, staring at his hands.

TELL ME YOUR HAPPIEST CHILDHOOD MEMORY
for Dot

In a house without a toybox,
everything felt like something.
Your mother's tweezers,
a plastic fork,
the lens from a broken pair of glasses.
You called this game gold-mining.

In the family room, combing the green shag rug
with your fingers, picking through the carpet
for sparkles fallen from the spackled ceiling,
you and your brothers and sisters knelt.

From oldest to youngest, you staked your claims
and gathered speck by speck
on hands and knees the glittering dust.
You raced the window's falling sun
until the darkened room gave out.

Then, your palm filled with gold,
more gold than anyone had ever found,
you sneaked into the hallway closet,
away from the others still digging for more,
and you held up to your eyes
that spark and shimmer.
What goodness you mined
you lifted to your open mouth
and swallowed, secret, all of it.
That light still simmers in your blood.

Brief Guide to Happiness

We crawled on hands and knees
toward water. We parted the ancient grasses
hunting music.

       Beetles castanetted in the dust.
       Harmonics pinged
       the cricket sphere.

       A bullfrog strummed
       its washtub gut.

 Then, light.

     *

Remember how that host of angels
landed in the trees—
shook out their wings
like snowy owls, how their breath
above our house whorled up
like chimney smoke,
and their wild coyote eyes,
their howling mouths.

     *

In a forest clearing,
a woman's soft hands
blindfolded us with kerchiefs,
turned us in circles, and said
now, children,
find your way home.

*

Summer at the town dump:

> scavenger hunt through a heap
> of broken televisions,
> bent-wheeled bicycles,
> lampshades, faded magazines.

From the junkpile, you pulled a red accordion.

Out of its loose keys and water-stained bellows
> wheezed a flying trapeze,
> the glitter of a tightrope,
> elephants plume-capped and on parade,
> the ringmaster's coiled whip,
> a lion crouched on an oil drum,
> ready to jump.

Together, we marched
the dust trail home, dreaming
of the hoop's ignition.

*

Inside our flashlight beams,
we shaped our hands to shadows
on the wall:

        two birds in flight
        above the river,

        a moose dragging its antlers
        through low
        and blackened clouds,

        on a faraway hill,
        two small people
        staring at the moon.

PSALM FROM THE DOLLHOUSE

The hearth is cold. The mantle clock unchiming.
Piano locked and lidded in the den.
Windows shuttered, slack-hinged, bent.
Through grey slats, a fence of splintered pine,
shadows where the ivy greened and climbed
towards the attic bedroom's unmade bed.
Pitched in corners and under chairs, cobweb
dust, moth husk, old flies. Nothing left alive.

Reach down a hand to set things right in me.
Room by room, sweep through. Make true the crooked door.
Gather up the figure lying facedown on the floor,
and blow the ashes from her eyes. Let her see
the table's feast. Let her drink. Let her eat
and then walk singing to the star-washed street.

Oh Ye of Little Faith

Waves still push upon the shore.
The moon's tidal drag, constant.
Instead of building up, the urge
to dig down settles in, the hands
pull back the earth, plumb the pit
to find out, yes, there, the water
wells up, too. Even in a gull's
warble, I hear the sea, and when
to the pillow I lay my head,
the little canals meander
to city lulled by gondolas,
and a man who calls to me
from his place on the water,
amore, amore.

Found Between the Pages

Of all that could have fallen—
origami swan,
wing of a red glider moth, torn
edge of a letter signed *Regretfully*,
photo of a shirtless white-haired man
waving goodbye—
of all that could have fallen
and been found in the high and lonely stacks
of the late night library,
out into my hands fell Christ—
the Saviour on a postcard,
his meek head crowned with thorns
and turquoise sheen.

He looked at me, content
in his unearthing, no doubt
aware I'd fallen too
from some small height and hiding place.

Whoever left him pressed into obscurity,
whoever ditched him like an awkward crush,
sent back to me a little crux of hope.

Around me strangers bent their heads
in study carrels, lost in terminology and fact.
Wind shook the skylights, outside
thrashed the courtyard's shedding maples.

Everything falling comes to rest.
In the wasteland of another cruel month
and far from home, I caved
to sign and symbol, white-flagged
against a shelf of modern poems
whose words went dust between the pages.

I held that paper childhood ghost
come back to haunt, his eyes
omniscient, his face toward me
unsettling what I knew—
a dry leaf pressed
and from me, shaken loose.

II.

MORNING PRAYER

With the cumbersome body I have been given,
I drag the mat into the circle of light that shines on the tile.

I kneel in the only posture I know to be true:
forehead to the bathroom floor,
hands pressed flat against the coolness.
As low to earth as I can get.

I try to think the thoughts of a snail and a saint at the same time.
I lick dust from stones. I float.

Forgive me, Lord. I judge too easily the faults of others,
including the neighbour lady who every morning
on her way to work backs onto my lawn.
Tire marks in the chewed-up sod—
the condition of my heart these days.

All famous mystics lived in stone abbeys or thatched-roof cottages.
They spoke a holy lexicon. They knelt in the soft moss of thickets
and prayed among fox and squirrel, beheld visions
of starry doves and wild clouds.
Last night in my dream, a black pig chased me
down a wooden flight of stairs.
Tell me, Lord, how do I read the spirit's restless typos?
And why must I live among groomed shrubbery,
the safe borders of pansy and primrose?

I've never been prone to long days of sadness, never dwelled
in the woodshed of despair more than a few smoky hours,
but lately, the routine of my wake and sleep, rise and fall,
aches inside me like a splintered rib, a broken tooth,
the voice of my mother in winter calling
when are you coming home?

In the morning, I bend to a God shadowed by my own stupidity.
In the evening, I sink into the alien water of dreams.
My flesh is grass and my body, the bucked-up jack pine
waiting for the burn.

Oh Lord, let me, like one who treks the frozen river
of discontent, come into a clearing sheltered from wind,
and in the drift and cold, kneel to gather fuel,
dry branches pruned from the tree,
let me scratch a flame from stone
and set the snow on fire, let me lift my hands
over the altar's smoke and incense, and with the ashes,
let me spark, with the ashes, let me rise.

To the Orb-Web Spider Outside My Working Window

Sun pins your shadow to my desk
where your black magnified shape
quivers above my writing hand.

You are the pencil's spectre
and any words that slide along the paper
belong to your spinning urge, not mine.

When I write *violence*, the strands of your web
bend like a mouth in the morning wind.
Write *desire* and your spinnerets

fire silk at the bluebottle's lazy
thrashing. Nothing I say sounds new.
Cranefly, mudwasp, mosquito, midge.

You spindle your eight legs, turning
each catch to a dusky cocoon
until your home's a hanging mausoleum.

On this side, the dead in me shift,
lift their veils, wait. Memory,
the stone I roll and roll away.

Highway 16 Sonnet

for Donna Kane

All summer long I walked a stretch of road
called hazardous by locals. Trucks flew past
(the posted speed limit a joke), loaded
up with wood, junk, flammables, and fastened
to the gas. Every week, at least one new
creature hit the ditch or shoulder, was hit
and hurled, fur and blood, next to some lost shoe
or bottle in shards. I counted on it,
needed that mess of beauty to send me
back to the empty room with something to say.
Dog, cat, rabbit, squirrel, fox, crow—debris
of a wilder gutted kingdom, decaying
with the kind of grace I've come to envy—
honest, splayed out for the world to see.
That kind of death I understand. Easy.
It's the other I can't take, the in-between,
like the doe that waited on the roadside
for her wobbling fawn with its wrecked backbone
and muzzle dripping red. It struggled, tried
to walk, fell down. I kept moving towards home
where the page waited. You know how it goes.
Words faltered, dragged, then from the dirt, they rose.

Elegy

O dead Canada goose,
ditched and rainbeaten
off the side of the road—
feet curled to the grey pillow
of your body like black bent
question marks asking
what happened?

A daredevil break from
your arrowhead gang yielded
the possibility of anywhere.
No leader but yourself,
no map but the blood's instinct—
then the head-on low-blow
of a garbage truck's high beams,
crush of feathers on glass.

Upside-down Icarus, you
flew too close to earth,
toward a sun doubled-over and false.
Now your sockets
tunnel oil. Your beak
fractures to a tongue
coal and bloated.

Above a tangle of brown grasses
winter's hexagon ignites.
Somewhere over a reedy bog
your broken vee is touching down,
blank-brained to the gap,
while you, wild smoke, climb
featherless into frost and blue.

Melancholy

Sometimes the fog's so thick, your eyes feel dipped
in smoke, or cloud, or ocean haze. Each day
you ride the sea, captain of your own slave ship.
Skeleton crew, mutiny, betrayal—
the murmurings deep in the hold rise up.
Your spyglass warps and blurs, your compass fails;
the threat of rougher water drains your cup
to dregs. You dream the belly of a whale,
and you inside that red cathedral gloom,
on your knees and begging God to let you
stay, darker here and safe, a cloistered womb
like where you started from, all blood and blues.
Who knew despair would drag you out this far,
then leave you drifting, searching for a star.

Metamorphosis

Under the whitewash of a moon, you stand
in a silver poplar forest hung with dolls,
same ones that stared you down in bedroom darkness
with their glossy, china eyes. There you light
the trees ablaze. There you witness holy colours,
that hidden spectrum of resentment turned
to flying ash, ruby, Venus, violet—
everything you ever wanted has come true.
All the blackened scales fall from your eyes
and then, and then, you kneel beneath that smoke.
You scrape the blood, dust, teeth and bone
into a pile smaller than your fist,
breathe on it until it changes shape—
a storybook, a mended clock, a mirror
breaking the blue sea back to sand and salt.

Metaphysic

The cove rock blackens
against scatterings of shell—
bleached arrowheads,
flint-tooth shards
that whiten in the sun.

The clam's slick meat, an oyster's gloss—
broken out of brackish water, clutched,
circled high in aerial maneuver,
then dropped
by crows and gulls
to crack the prey
and free the fuel inside.

Who doesn't crave
the battering and blows,
forge and bellows,
crucible for gold?

The child who drags her finger
through the flame
grows up and snuffs the candle
with a pinch.

All flesh is grass,
and stone, and wood, and smoke.
The end of things foreseeable as rain.

Today the sun burns hard.
The sea pulls back its skin.

On this rock, I lay my body out
for good, for grief,
for demolition's sweet ride
towards relief.

Last Night in a Dream
for Colleen

You came to me as a peacock,
yelling like a woman
hung from a balcony ledge.

I wore the white dress of childhood,
you the old Victorian plumage,
the turquoise vest of a vaudeville star.

We always were thrown together,
oddly matched in a world
that favours symmetry.

From the ruined apple tree,
you stared across twilight
with the omniscience of

a technicolour myth.
I knelt, pressed my forehead
to wet grass, stones.

God, on the fifth day, created
you and all your kind,
dipped your bones in the sea,

and over your feathers breathed
one hundred luminous ways
of looking at the earth.

No wonder when you saw me
you called for help, knowing
what it means to be rescued

from nothing, knowing how
the voice flies up from the heart,
green-winged and brooding

over the lost art of humility,
that old dream, old prayer
shaking off the dust.

MEDITATION ON PRAYER

A wire strung through air
and various moons,
through seraphim, Hyperion,
the rare blood star of morning.

A strand of the priest's
white hair, floating
in the nave.

And the bell-ringer's reach,
and the rope,
and the bell.

A cord of fire dragged
through water, ire,
sapphire.

Heretic anchored in the lake
off the shore of yearning.

Under a grey and granite rain
I tear words from the page—
feather, paper, feather.

PROLOGUE

Tell Him you forgot which tree—
you thought the orange off-limits,
or the fig. So many kinds,
it's hard to keep them straight. Say
you guessed His threat a joke—who, us?
Keep smiling when you see Him.
Like nothing's come between.
Find out the angel's weakness.
Sweet-tooth? Flattery?
What's the going rate
on bribery? Tell Him how
that serpent pinwheeled, curlicued
your name in scales at your feet.
You never meant to swallow,
never meant to take a bite—
you slipped, tripped on a root, the fruit
near slid into your mouth.
What's the difference
between one tree and a forest
full of lookalikes? There,
inside the garden, our view
was skewed by so much light,
the sun shimmying off pools,
needling the eye. Even now
the sword-blade's scorch
throws out fire like a trick.

Our lashes singe. Our cheeks burn.
When we tip the palm leaf
to our lips, water's low. No rain.
Gnarled roots and sand. We walk on
flaying stones. Ask Him
how much longer do we wait
for Him to change
His mind, let us in to
try again, this time for good.

DIVINING

I.

It was the devil in my hands
that set the willow trembling.
That's what the elders preached.
No witching here, they said,
and stood on holy ground, unmoving.

Yet the river, low that summer,
brought them to their knees
praying rain. *Lord, let the farmers' crops
rise up green and wither not.*
.Their tongues were dust.

II.

Well by well, the pumps drew mud.
Cattle bloated at the fenceline.
In the air, the taste of chaff and smoke.
Behold, the preacher called up prophets,
behold. We sweat and wiped our brows.

A week of supplication and *oh ye of little faith*.
The sun pitched an apocalyptic sheen.
Into the fields, the men dragged
burlap soaked to beat down fires
sparking in the heat.

III.

The earth is the Lord's and the fullness thereof,
that much the elders admitted, but warily,
warily brought me in, and stood back still
as if the forked branch held out
were the very serpent's tongue.

Behind the church, they followed,
paces back lest any gypsy trickery leach off.
The phantom root, remembering its source,
began to quiver. Strike here, I said,
and crouched to scuff an X into the dirt.

IV.

They couldn't dig. No one would man the auger.
Repentance and a mustard seed of faith is all we need.
In the end, the proverb ruled.
The minister lofted the scriptures
and at the pulpit, red-faced, rallied.

Men again burned decks of cards and radios,
and women wept for wayward sons and daughters.
The tribe called down their manna in the wilderness.
Water from a rock more ancient than the dirt —
that's what they wanted.

V.

What tremor in the dowsing rod I felt
was deep and calling deep, tuned
to find its given key. Even stones can sing.
Stars, too. Why not in harmony, underground,
the spring and stream a tonic to the root?

Late summer, at the river, they baptized
in a shallow current, kneeling for the full immersion.
When the preacher bent to bring each body up,
those on shore raised high their trembling hands
and shouted hallelujah, praise God from whom all blessings flow.

Summer Afternoon, Lying in the Grass

Now is the time for the book to lie folded
over my chest, words breathing
against my ribcage, little mouths
that fog and cloud my body's slatted windows.

Bearded professors with their
thin and scribbling pencils say
the house is the metaphor for the soul.

But not today. Today,
my body is the house.

Wind lifts the kitchen curtains,
blows through the bedroom.
Sunlight filters motes
that hang above quiet furniture,
these bones.

Let the wakeful self gather what it needs,
lug its travel bags to the threshold,
lock the door behind,
swallow the key.

As I pass, I glance back
through glass to see what's left—
darkening empty rooms,
ashes cooling in the hearth,
and the sky's mirror behind
letting down a white ladder.

Music for Dead Children

Glass bell swinging
in an attic window. Ivory
chimes that hang inside
a storm. Half-sized violin,
sousaphone, silver whistle
on a string, June bug swarm.

Mothwing-strumming
in an old tin pail. Shale
skipped out across a boatless lake—
there, there, there. Rain
ticking, pin-drop, on a snail shell.
Slide-wire over sand, a garter snake.

The dusk train's steam and clatter,
echo-call to cuckoo clock
and glockenspiel. Sigh
of candlesmoke along a sill.
Hollyhock drowsed and scoured
by a lone sawfly.

The playground's milk moon
climbs through mist and rain,
calling down shadows
from their swinging chains.

BIRTHDAY

Still you wake with a fishy feeling
in your gut, that swim of zip and flicker.
Yes, it's just another day, but part of you
half-expects a headline announcing
the anniversary of your arrival here on earth.

At your age, neighbourhood kids
don't circle the dining room table
for an after-school party.
Your permed and aproned mother
doesn't enter the room with a cake
in the shape of a stegosaurus
spiked with gumdrops,
its spinal plates blazing sparklers.
You wear no pointed paper hat.
Now, dignity coordinates
your belt and polished shoes.

The chorus of squawking noisemakers
blown until their rainbow paper drips with spit
has faded to a radio's monotonous weather.
The backyard of blindfolded children
attacking the air with a sawed-off broomstick
has emptied to a balding hedged-in lawn.

Today there is no silver dollar pancake breakfast
steaming on the counter, no stack
of presents to unwrap.

You lock the front door behind
and head into the work life has given.
Some gift. Some party.

The sun over your sidewalk,
a solitary, loose balloon,
floats up through trees
in a sky wrapped cloudless blue.

On the telephone wire that sags above your head,
a gang of crows suits up for morning,
slicking their black feathers, calling out
through traffic rush the day's minor news.

Custom Caskets Made to Order

We trade our dying wishes back and forth
like travel plans each summer as we pass
the road sign advertising custom caskets.

Highway 97 heading north, the billboard
guarantees to give your loved one honour
in a wooden coffin made to order,
adorned with ancient pictograms on pine,
inlaid with cedar for a striking design, or
carved plain in a spirit of humility,
suitable for folks with simple taste.

We banter modes of burial, the if and how—
ashes mixed with oil paints and brushed into a sunset,
a bath in liquid nitrogen, then shaken to a powder,
converti-coffin doubling as an entertainment stand.

Utilitarian, he wants whatever's cheapest:
cardboard in a bonfire, compost in the flowerbed,
who cares, I'm dead, chuck me in the kiln.
Every year I counter with the hometown family plot,
imagining my predecessors waiting in a root cellar
around a card table, playing Rook. Black suits.
Black dresses. That's where I want to be, however dank.

More years together than apart, our threshold wears.
Trouble sleeping when he isn't there,
and when he is, eternity's a sad idea,
a ghost town without him waking next to me.

In the Cariboo country we drive through,
motel vacancies blaze their neon no's.
So much love, it's hard to think ahead.
Like how the signs we pass predict the rest
kilometres away. Abstract in the distance,
the next small town grows closer
with houses row on row, narrow streets,
and on the other side of the river,
across the bridge, a fenced and tended cemetery
mowed weekly through the summer.

Ars Domestica

Evening ritual brings us side by side
at the kitchen sink, you with your snapping dishtowel
and me with the soapy cloth and scrubber.

Since the beginning, it's been this way,
me washing down the apparatus of the day,
wood and bone, iron and glass,
while you finish what I begin.

Omega of my domestic alphabet,
full-stop at the end of my rambling sentence —
tonight, I want to die before you,
be the first one to slip into those silvery waters and swim away,

while you stand shore-bound, a little helpless,
but still holding onto that white towel, ready
to take up the final chores of living.

No superstitions here. Only cotton sheets,
a summer quilt, the practicality of flesh,
but say I'm the kind of girl to believe in the magic
of midsummer's eve. Say I frisk through twilight
fields of grasses named for flame and fountain,
blue hair, plume and eyelash—
say I chant their Latin names like invocation.

Hem of my dress weighed down by dew,
of course I grow faint, of course I sink into a meadow,
lie in a rush of blossom with my hair halo-wheeled
in the lilies and violets. In the brook that riffles over stone,
in the nightingale's purple flute, I only hear your name.

When the swirled moon rises, I draw a circle
in its light, float home to place beneath my pillow
a twine-wrapped fist of lavender and sage,
and yes, I fall to dreaming of you, the one
to whom I've sewn my flesh and bone
with oath and candlelight.

But too bad it's me, your ordinary wife
who crawls in next to you with hands like ice
and even colder feet, who sidles up for warmth
and catalogues the common day:
ten quail in the ditch this morning,
a letter in the mail, white blossoms
in the orchard apple trees.

Summer's coming, I whisper in your ear.
The moon drips down its honey,
and up the road, in the white pine frames
of the farmer's apiary,
the bees sleep two by two
in cells of gold.

READING IN BED

Tonight he's locked in a book on contemporary economics
and I'm cruising someone else's hotrod poems.

We drive this familiar stretch of road
stuck in separate lanes, a crease the length

of our bodies marking sides of the bed.
He holds his place, steady on the turns,

he gears down for the signs.
When he slides his hand onto my thigh,

it's a signal, he's headed for the exit,
city nightlife, neon throbbing smoke and song.

I flip ahead another page, shift into the passing lane,
rev up for the chase. Who knows

how dark the tunnel, how slippery the bridge?
Who knows how tight the hairpin curves ahead?

Waking on the Moon

Morning rises like a dust bath. What little wind there is
sifts around our ankles as we walk the regolith.

When you reach for my hand, it's a weightless grip.
Every crater looks like the one before.

After *Blue Moon, Moon River, Fly Me to the Moon,*
I expected more than this.

Why, when we finally reach the dream,
does the destination fall short? Hope, a spent rocket.

Back home we passed cool evenings huddled
in blankets on the porch, lulled by this phase.

Now the sky's a gutted neighbourhood—
black holes and broken glass of dying stars.

Planets flush and sag like paper lanterns
we once hung to celebrate the night

in that backyard party of our vintage life,
when we walked the dewy lawn together,

picking up the empties in the dark.

Sunday Morning in the Park

While our dogs in the wetness of morning grass
nose each other back to front and sniff out histories,
the man tells me of his wife's affair,
her strange perfume, late-night telephone calls,
how they still sit down to dinner
every night, wash the dishes side by side,
how after the kids fall asleep, he moves
across the hall to the hide-a-bed,
makes sure to be the first awake and fold away
his blankets, tidy up, but then this morning,
his daughter rises early, finds him
stumbling from the guest room, wonders why
he's not in his own bed, and so he calls it
sleepwalking, says he sometimes finds himself
awake in strangeness, lost
in his own house. This bleak-eyed man
in t-shirt and pajama pants confesses
he's no good at breaking vows,
what can he do?

I've come prepared for weather chat,
the *hey there how are you*, hands-in-pockets
talk of average rainfall, lack of sun,
those common distance rituals,
not the space between us closed
with sudden intimacy.

The art of empathy is hard to master,
hard to fake. To make compassion rise
from the heart's bare suburbs, to stutter
alongside the sufferer, lost art. Whatever
words I say go useless in the air,
silk flowers at the bedside of the sick.

I check my watch. He whistles for his dog
to come, back to the biscuit
in his open hand, and to the leash.

III.

Hymn for Night

Dream-hearse, moon-shackle,
scarecrow mausoleum. Maroonland.
Silken ether handkerchief.

Nocturne looping on a gramophone,
Persephone's telegram,
epigram of the apocalypse.

Hope in a hooded cloak.
Ghost-weather, bone-cocoon.
Cab ride to the afterlife.

Graveyard of the firefly.
Factory of desire, the sea darkly thinking,
tinderbox of shadow.

Cistern of the weeping prophet,
the spirit's mending table,
the body's whetstone.

Ancient riddle inkwell,
a sealed letter yet unsent,
sky of cancelled words.

The tremble in the bridegroom's hands.
That held breath after
the virgin's lamp goes out.

CALLING THE STARS

Every star that wheels
on glittered spokes
through blackness—

every knothole,
pawprint, glint of glass
through trees, raccoon's eye,

firefly and fish's mouth,
arrowhead, nested egg, pennies
tossed above the creek,

magnolia leaf and flung in handfuls,
bluegrass seed, wind chime
spark and garden bell

to swing against
the sprinkler's silver arc
of rain—

every star a tallied name
called home to night's dark porch,
above a flowerbed of shadows,

shining there, a girl's lost earring
fallen down in quartz
and blossom,

where through the open window
play the piano's
high white keys.

LEARNING HOW TO PRAY
after Antonio Machado's "Memory from Childhood"

A clear, wet sun in June.
We stand inside the greenhouse
glass and heat, dark and dirt.

Above me hang the trowel and the rake,
the baler twine and chicken wire,
implements of work.

My mother dips a paintbrush tip
inside a yellow flower, then lifts its dust
and touches it inside another bloom.

She moves from plant to plant
in her blue dress, quiet
as a Sunday afternoon,
entering this slow vocation
meant to yield fruit.

A clear, wet sun in June.
We stand inside the greenhouse
glass and heat, dark and dirt.

LOVE POEM

My mother's crying tugs
us from our bunkbeds
and sleep's watery shadows
to where she lies on the sofa
with her face pressed into
a cushion's embroidered roses.

Her hair hangs over her face.
One strap of her nightgown
has fallen down her shoulder.
Her body shakes with quiet sobs.

Over her, my father leans
with a hand laid upon her head.
He drags long on his cigarette,
then blows smoke
into her ear.

When she moans like something
lost and wandering in the trees out back,
he breathes another hot mouthful
into her pain, tells her
never mind what doctors say,
this will fix any ache,
give it a chance.

Barefoot, my brother and I
stand in our pajamas on the threshold.
All the good intentions of our lives
meet here, in the middle of the night,
on the edge of the living room,
where love tries and tries
again, hangs its head over us
and promises a cure
for all that hurts.

My Father in Heaven

Every dog he's ever shot,
every cat torn away by raven or owl,
every pig butchered come September,
every chicken whose head he axed,
every moose strung and quartered
in the woodshed, every deer
he gutted by the fire—

in heaven, they all gather around my father
like lambs to a lion. He sits
on a block of wood just inside the gates,
with the animals come to lick
his smooth, un-yellowed hands.

He touches his left shirt pocket, habit,
finds it empty, but the jitters
never come and his blood keeps steady
and the sun is everywhere, but it's
still cool enough for long sleeves
and a down-filled hunting vest.

The wind brings the smell of wild strawberries
and cream, and he hears his mother
singing in German, and his father
whistling from the raspberry canes,
and the collie that slept beneath his bed
turns in circles at his feet,

and finally he remembers
the answer to that math problem
from his grade seven exam, the last one
he took before leaving school
to work Uncle Bill's dairy farm.

Then my mother in her nightgown
descends a staircase to bring him a glass of milk,
and he's wearing his long johns
and someone has laid a steel guitar
across his lap, and his hands, new hands,
they know how to play
all the old hymns he left behind,
and this time, they sound like new songs
because everyone is singing,
even his daughter and his son,
they stand beside him now,
dressed in his old work clothes
with gold flecks of sawdust falling
from their hair because they've come
from chopping and stacking all that wood
he hauled out of the bush, all that wood he hauled
to build those winter fires, his daughter and his son,
they come from finishing
all the work he meant to do,
and they come singing,
singing like they mean it.

Waking to Eternity

Not light you notice first,
but green
shoots and tendrils
winding up the bones,
what were your bones,
and leafprints pressed against
your skin,
what was your skin.

So this is how to think
two worlds at once—

how it is evening
with a white moth
drinking from the pool
of a low moon,

how it is horses
disappearing into the hayfield,
leaving the sun
and a trail of dust behind.

Postcard from New Earth

No busying in fire and ice. No need
to cage the panther from the dove.

The difficult to reconcile
ride beside the Sea of Glass
on tandem bicycles.

Monkeys wander freely
next to angels in the park.

The dumb conduct
the multitudes in song.

To say I wish you were here
would be a lie: longing
is a verb continuing in the present
never reaching for the past.

On an isthmus of white sand,
beneath a sunrise-sunset tango,
I'm folding a paper boat,
I'm sailing it off the edge to you
who back home labours
in weedy garden heat,
who digs out morning glory roots
beside a pond of sluggish koi.

Together with a cloud of witnesses,
I'm soloing a breathy riff
across the water, love,
to blow away the blackflies
and cool your sweaty brow.

Ad Infinitum

All things, not only good, come to an end,
except infinity, that racetracked helix
knotting alpha to omega, an Escher loop
of sunrise-sunset tricking out the mind—
imagine God, hunkered down and tinkering
with a clock the size of Texas but beautiful;
no edgy bomb-tick quartzing under glass;
instead, a dozen angels water-fluting
liquid light, barometric in their whirling
through cloud, carnelian and jasper;
no seconds wrenched, no screwdriven hours,
no itchy wristwatch snagging at the skin—
ah, this is how I want my time to pass—
bolted to a higher vantage point,
ecstatic in the spinning, cogs and wheels
ditched for a weathervaning mind,
a soulish wind, blowing north, south, east, west.

Ode to a Ghost Pipefish

Look for a ghost pipefish
and you will see how
the faithful see, what
game they play. A coral reef
and ocean floor, the sea's
mud-bottomed weeds
and waterscape of rays
(both sun and sting)—
these trick the hunter's eye.
You think you see
the creature spread its fins?
An optical illusion's
what you find—a sway of kelp
or mangrove floating in
your gaze. What's vision
but a dreamy haze gone clear?
Breath, a strand of pearls
cut loose and rising, disappears.
Falling scales glitter down
your glassy dark. That fishy ruse
unnerves like anything unseen
but near, a lure dragging you
through this world down here.

APOLOGETIC

And then a little wind blows through,
enough to morph the leafy skyline,
ruffle the morning flight path of a bird.

A cutthroat up from water flings its silver filings
to the sun—zing of metal, vanishing
harmonics back inside the lake's blaze.

The lines between up there, down here
cross-hatch and blur, razor the veil.
The forest wicks up fungal, emerald,

fuelled sub-terrain with carbon songs
that swell in oil, roots, stars.
Even stones, licked clean by rain

and blackly lit, conspire to uncloud my eye.
Re-tool my mind. I'm back at the beginning,
squinting on the fringe of beauty's rootwork,

myopic and in love. I know full well
my notes are crude. Loose keys.
Scrawlings from a stick I drag in sand.

Slant of a wing. Loop of petals. Outline
of a fish on land. A tracery the wind picks up
and sifts, shifting the ground I stand on.

At the End of the Dock

The sun lays down its silver avenue.
The anchored sailing boat's
white paint and chrome
blindfolds a dazzled flash across my eyes.

What was my body, a breathless raft,
bobs off, flotsam in the slack.
What used to be my feet
lift from grit and splinter.

All other dreams of passage—
night chase tunnel,
fiery ladder dropped from clouds,
that basement slideshow
of yesterday on yesterday—
they lose their brilliance here.

What used to be sky's blue infinity,
the end, *ad infinitum*—
what used to be drops off
in darkness, fathoms past a fishhook moon,
the copper eyelids of the stars.

Up through a sea of light,
and lighter still, what used to be
my bones climb up,
rise into after-light,
shadowless and dripping.

INVOCATION
Calling all butterflies of every race . . . —ROBERT FROST

Come monarch, spice-bush, sleepy orange,
come broken silverdrop.

Syllabic mist, come ruby-spotted,
mourning cloak, cabbage white.

Antithesis of Armageddon's
blasted sky and bloody moon

is a haze of you, cloudless sulphur,
firestorm of daggerwing,

armada of mimosa yellow,
pearly marble, metalmark.

Come southern dogface, dark kite,
common buckeye, cattleheart.

Every tribe, nation, tongue
including yours, that thread

by which you sew yourself
to milky bloom on bloom,

where you drink, wavering,
then unstitch and fly to light,

your wings, confessing
the flimsy dust and paper,

your lifting, argument against
the former body's dew and silk.

Dear John on the Island of Patmos

It's not you, it's Him—that Other you call
Love who slips gems down to you, fills your head
like a glittering cave until you see
what others won't. Or can't. I've seen that look—
mercury eyes owling in the pitch.

Beneath the backyard olive tree, on your knees
outside the window, you'd grope for holds,
tin-tongued, fiddle with your ragged prayer shawl,
tap code with a nail on stone. Lick your thumb
and lift it to wind. Listen, you'd say,
it's blowing in, it's coming close, He's here.

Then an imperceptible smattering
of rain. Three bleats from a neighbour's sheepfold.
A skull-sized cloud drifting overhead. Signs,
you revelled, celestial pictograms etched
by heaven's hand. You saw them everywhere.

Wait, you said and said again—He starts small,
comes like a cricket on a barley spike,
gold on gold and singing barely—listen.
And I tried to tune my ear to water
humming in a well, to hear what you hear.

But my heart's been riddling hard since we met.
When in the early hours you came home
and sank into our bed, a heat fanned off
your unlike flesh and stoked in me a green flame.
While you slept, your smile held a whetstone
to my dulling knife. Things murmured I couldn't
understand. What kind of sullen wife
could nurse a bruise like this? I'd brood and hate
my life, this staring through a burlap sack.

Now your disciples bring little news, say only
your writing hand grows weak with revelation,
your face shines more each time they see you,
and by the way, you send your love, post-script.

The clipping from your beard and frayed tassel
torn from your robe, I've tacked to our threshold
like you asked. Pilgrims limp in every day to touch
what you have touched, make relics of your cells.
Palsied hands untremble. Milky eyes go clear.
They call out blessings from the doorway
but I stay dumb. Pretend I can't hear
the way you hear, see the way you see.
In my heart, I kick our boundary stone
far as the sea that crashes at your cave.
You know what's on God's mind. Why not mine?

Come read me like an exile's torchlit scroll.
Come see me now, standing at the birdcage
where your solitary parakeet swings and whistles
for its morning seeds and figs, waiting
for a hand to come, slip the twig door's latch.

Backyard Birding with St. Francis

Junco. Grackle. Rufus-sided towhee.
Each one that comes to feed
from my oak tree's swinging suet cage,
he classifies. Whether dark-throated trill,
crown of chestnut feathers, chewinking
red-eyed chirp—he knows them all
quirk by quirk, like old Apostle Paul knew
Yahweh's law, aleph, bet and gimel.

The flicking scripture of their tongues,
nimble-footed scrollwork in the dirt,
their singing—ah, their singing—
no altar bell ringing comes close!

Winged illumination of the text, he says.
Hear it? The syrinx pipes what next
will be our hymns—their notes
before our verse, Creation ever prior to the curse.

We off-key warblers chant and liturgize,
but a sparrow, whistling
as it catches flies, lifts a cleaner canticle,
confessing nothing but its sparrowness.
What's blessing but a creature doing
what it's made to do?

He plucks a grass blade, blows
a green screak through the slit,
playing back a nuthatch cry.

And then he's on his knees, pointing
at the sky—Look up! Turkey vulture!
Cathartes aura: purifier of dead fauna
and flora field-rotting in the Latin and the Greek;
bird without a vocal cord, can't speak
except to hiss and grunt, but watch it ride
the air's current, how fluently it glides!

And I do. A winged V above my head,
a folio thumbed open, floating,
read by wind and reading wind.

What's reading me?
St. Francis mimics *chickadee-dee-dee*
to the black-capped acrobats
that twitch branch to twig, twig to branch,
chitter and scritch-scratch in sawdust,
flinging seed everywhere
as they carry on, singing.

THE NEW CONTINENT

I.

A wooden bridge, a stream of trout,
a single plum tree leaning to the east:

even through the palace window,
a man's world grows small; therefore—

under the silk map of a China sky,
Wan Hu, Ming dynasty official,

straps himself to a wicker chair,
and orders his servants to tie to his seat

47 bamboo tubes packed with gunpowder,
then light those fuses in unison.

Into the night, he's launched,
stars and confetti, blast of dragon scales

bright shreds of kite-tails fluttering
in a banner of smoke and torches, because

doesn't everyone ache to travel towards
what he does not know, toward that other

fishing village hooked to the moon,
to the dark idea of its ocean?

II.

A week before her eightieth birthday,
my grandmother buys a violin.

On the kitchen windowsill
lined with ripening tomatoes,

she props a how-to book with photos
of a younger woman holding another violin,

a mirror of how her knotted hands might look
with decades smoothed away.

Soundboard. Ribs. Neck. Scroll. She learns
the instrument's anatomy edgework to fret,

slides her fingers down those razor tightropes
and over the bow's horsehair scratch

that brings her back to the Kansas farm
of childhood: fenceline, milk bucket, firewood

unlike the shape her hands now grip,
this maple flame carved from a tree

in a forest she has never walked through
noting birdcalls in a foreign tongue.

Like the book suggests, she balances the bow
on open G, first step into high-wire blackness

stretching between here and the Blue Danube,
that castle-waltzing far-off river.

III.

After hauling your nets up empty from the silt,
you sail on in your makeshift boat

of skin and paper, catch what wind you can
until the new continent appears.

You drag yourself to shore, water-heavy,
compass-weary, stunned by the air's

violet and humming machine.
What you have come for greets you now

with a generosity that humbles;
fish leap like handfuls of silver

coins tossed from the surf.
Fire waits inside a circle of stones. Sparks

rise orange on black to butterfly the night.
You lift your eyes to an unordinary horizon:

vines shot through with birdsong, fruit
hanging whole notes in the trees.

Into that jungle of leaves and music
you set out, a trail of nameless flowers

before you and above,
the sky's new alphabet of stars.

SHADOW LAKE

Birch in autumn shock reflect themselves—
in paradox the elements go head to head;
fire shimmers deep within the water.

You say, well look at that
and whistle through your teeth,
hook your thumbs in belt loops,
shake your head.

Wonder is a posture
held in low esteem.
The greenness of the world,
commodity. How odd
the trees once fall
has polished them to bone.
How odd.

Who owns the coming snow?
Where in God's name
can a person go
to duck the noise?

By now, your clothes shucked off
and ditched in dirt, you're in
up to your neck, treading
in the mountain runoff,
in the mirror of the sky:

you, yourself
reflective,
swimming in the shock
of autumn's birch.

MINK

Slip of ink and curl of fur,
oil slick under the sun,
not you, mercurial
among the lilies,
but the one
who thinks you up
to whom a psalm
quicksilvers in my gut.

Trinket-eyed you slink the lake,
and, pilfering the drink, lift
rivet-jawed from the water's fringe
a steely smolt.

And though your teeth
wink quartz in smithereens,
and your claws with knack and skill
split gill to gill the skin from rib,
you are the magician's silk
that lifts the trick to light,
but not the light.

A glinty hook, you are
another lure that jigs
the deepward eye:
go sing.

DESIGN

I found beside the trail a jilted nest
spilling out three eggs in shards, blue, sparrowless.
Woven twig and moss, braided cord—
the kind that tugs a child's hood on tight—
and too, dog hair, feather down, dryer lint,
a burlap thread or two. This patchy nest
flown in, packed and tatted: home concoction
hoisted straight from the brain of a bird,
begun as lacework in the blood, instinct
lightboxed in cells. Words, too, blow down this road—
scrap, cast-off as a broken string, a fist
of wayside, weedy fuzz. I bent to see
the builder's scheme: odds, ends. Whatever's found,
lifted, and in the lifting, made fit.

Ring Around the Moon

I drag the late night garbage
across the driveway and the moon
accosts: open-mouth high note,
whole note of a moon.

Stars blink back their wonder.
Startled faces with a smatter
of applause, ovation
for the celestial elite.

Below, I lug the junk,
heave the raccoon-proof
plywood up from the bins,
dump the stench and re-lid.

We carry out our chores.
Shine. Schlep. Two tones
on the same dark scale,
a chord of dissonance.

The haze of light, that ring
around the moon, haloes
out our song. Hallowed,
humbled, I bow, then carry on.

REFINERY

Let Saint George have his dragon,
Saint Francis, his birds.

I want Cecilia's final hours
and her chamber of sweat,

to be unfettered, to take the noose,
the stake, cauldron and fire,

sunk down in the smelter like coal,
come up diamond,

to find the crucifix
a spine of gold inside,

sackcloth and angels,
bleeding and heat, I want

a cindered alphabet in Latin,
my blackened tongue still singing,

and the axe, when it falls, to cleave me
cleanly from this house.

~

TESTIMONY

A sheath of linen,
a parcel of silence, a withering
lily of the field, I was.

A calendar of dust and twigs.

Whitecap on the sea of in-between,
an ever-cresting wave
not cresting.

Like one shaded in the *plein-air*
of a picnic by the shore,
among figs and bread,
dry wineglasses,
my body rested still.

Cloud-minded, I was
unhurried in the afternoon's stalled light.
Hammocked in my bones.

Then, that voice
calling through stone
my name.

Acknowledgements

Some of these poems were written during my tenure as poet laureate for the City of Victoria. Many thanks to the Mayor and Council, and to the City staff, for the opportunity to fill this post.

Much appreciation to Turnstone Press, especially Sharon Caseburg for helping this manuscript find a shape and for her encouragement during the final revision weeks.

Thank you to my New Life family and to other communities of faith who encourage the artist and the arts.

A deep well of gratitude to my ever-excellent family, to Amelia, daughter extraordinaire, and to Lance, my love, my husband.

Above all, to the one who is able to keep me from falling, which is, I assure you, no small job.